EP Language Arts 6
Printables

This book belongs to:

_____

This book was made for your convenience. It is available for printing from the Easy Peasy All-in-One Homeschool website. It contains all of the printables from Easy Peasy's Language Arts 6 course. The instructions for each page are found in the online course.

Please note, in the various places where parts of speech are practiced, certain words can be categorized in more than one place (you can go for a swim [noun] or you can swim [verb]). If your child marks one of them differently than the answer key indicates, have a conversation with them to find out why.

Easy Peasy All-in-One Homeschool is a free online homeschool curriculum providing high quality education for children around the globe. It provides complete courses for preschool through high school graduation. For EP's curriculum visit allinonehomeschool.com.

EP Language Arts 6 Printables

ISBN-13: 978-1722912352
ISBN-10: 1722912359

First Edition: August 2018

Can you follow directions? Set a timer for 3 minutes — complete this worksheet within the allotted time!

1.   Read everything thoroughly before you do any step.
2.   Put your name in the top right corner of this page.
3.   Shout your first name.
4.   Circle the word "corner" in step 2.
5.   If you have followed the directions so far, yell "Yes!"
6.   In the blank space above number 1, write "I can!"
7.   Down the left margin, draw five circles.
8.   Put a check mark in each circle.
9.   Draw a square around each circle.
10. Say the alphabet out loud in order.
11. Count to ten out loud.
12. Count backwards from 10 to 1 out loud.
13. Use the bottom left section to divide 1089 by 11.
14. Circle your answer to number 13.
15. Shout, "I am the master of direction-following!"
16. Use the bottom right section to add $10,820$ to $3,999$.
17. Draw a triangle around your answer.
18. Draw a rectangle around the triangle.
19. Yell, "I'm almost done and have followed the directions!"
20. Underline all of the even numbers on the whole page.
21. Draw a line through step 14.
22. Now that you've read everything, only do steps 1 and 2!

Lesson 11: Metaphors

Answer the following questions as a refresher course on metaphors.

We could have people over more often if the *house wasn't such a pigsty*.

This metaphor compares the house to a pigsty because...

  a.   ...we raise pigs.
  b.   ...it stinks like a barn.
  c.   ...it is messy.

I woke up to a *blanket of snow* on the ground.

This metaphor compares the snow to a blanket because...

  a.   ...it covered the ground.
  b.   ...it was warm.
  c.   ...it was on the bed.

Emma's *legs were Jell-O* as she took her place on the stage.

This metaphor compares Emma's legs to Jell-O because...

  a.   ...she spilled her snack on them.
  b.   ...they were shaking from her nerves.
  c.   ...she was hungry.

Sam, *the family early bird*, got the rest of the cereal.

This metaphor compares Sam to an early bird because...

  a.   ...he liked worms.
  b.   ...he got up before everyone else.
  c.   ...he enjoyed singing in the morning.

Properly punctuate the dialogue at the top of the page. Then use the lines at the bottom of the page to copy the interesting quote by your historical person.

Come here he said

She got up and crossed the room What is it

A geode.

She asked again And that is what exactly

He brought out a hammer Watch and see.

Quote:_____

_____

_____

_____

Author: _____

Date written: _____

Source: _____

_____

(This page left intentionally blank)

Cut out the following pieces and arrange them into different dialogues. Don't forget to use the rules you've learned.

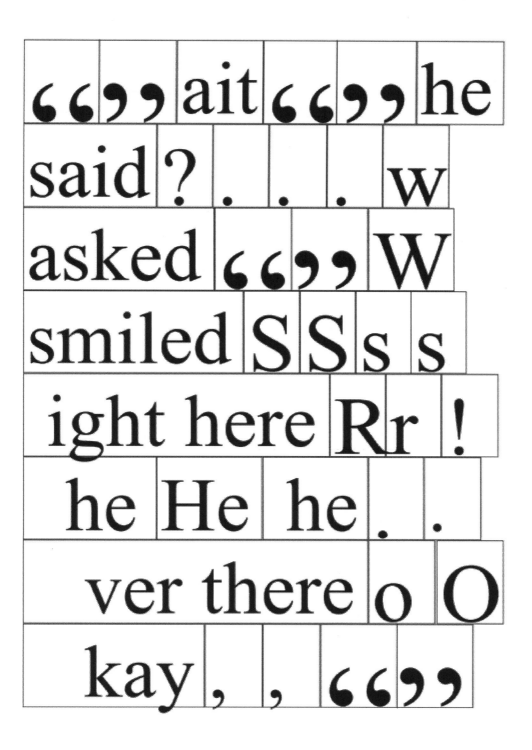

(This page left intentionally blank)

Lesson 53: Capitalization

Cut out as one piece. Fold in each side and crease. Cut along the dotted lines. Inside each flap write at least one example of each. (Name titles would be Aunt Jenny or President Obama, whereas titles would be aunt and president.)

common nouns things	places	prepositions and insignificant words in titles	titles	first word in the second part of an interrupted quote

Proper Nouns Names of Things	Names of Places	Significant Words in Titles (e.g. book titles)	Name Titles With Names or As Names	The First Word of a Quotation

(This page left intentionally blank)

Lesson 55: Comma Rules

Write an example of each rule on the line that follows it.

Rule #1 Use a comma to separate things in a series or list.

_____

Rule #2 Use a comma before a conjunction (and, or, but, so) when they separate independent clauses.

_____

Rule #3 Use a comma to separate introductory words in a sentence.

_____

Rule #4 Use a comma to set apart appositives and other unnecessary information.

_____

Rule #5 Use a comma to separate adjectives if you could say "and" in between them.

_____

Rule #6 Use a comma to separate quotes from speech tags.

_____

Rule #7 Use a comma to set apart phrases that express contrast.

_____

Rule #8 Use a comma to avoid confusion.

_____

Rule # 9 Use a comma between city and state, date and year.

_____

Rule #10 Never use only one comma between a subject and its verb.

_____

Refresh yourself on comma rules by correcting each sentence according to the rule that precedes it.

Rule #1 Use a comma to separate things in a series or list.

I used to ride bikes skip rope run races and roll in the grass.

Rule #2 Use a comma before a conjunction (and, or, but, so) when they separate independent clauses.

Now I cook and clean and my kids do all those things.

Rule #3 Use a comma to separate introductory words in a sentence.

When I was young I thought being old would be fun.

Rule #4 Use a comma to set apart appositives and other unnecessary information.

Now that I'm old as if thirty-seven is old I think I was right.

Rule #5 Use a comma to separate adjectives if you could say "and" in between them.

I have a bunch of fun energetic creative kids.

Rule #6 Use a comma to separate quotes from speech tags.

"It's tomorrow" my son says in the mornings.

Rule #7 Use a comma to set apart phrases that express contrast.

We try and explain that it's today not tomorrow.

Rule #8 Use a comma to avoid confusion.

He'll jump up and say, "Let's eat Mom!"

Rule # 9 Use a comma between city and state, date and year.

We haven't lived near Philadelphia Pennsylvania since May 31 2002.

Rule #10 Never use only one comma between a subject and its verb.

Riding a bike is something you never forget how to do.

Lesson 64: Editing Checklist

Read through your essay and fix any mistakes. Here is an editing checklist. Aim for a check mark in each box.

Introduction

☐ My introduction begins with an attention grabber.
☐ My introduction has at least three sentences.
☐ My introduction ends with the main idea of my essay.

Body

☐ The body of my essay has at least three paragraphs.
☐ Each paragraph of the body starts with a topic sentence.
☐ Each paragraph of the body has at least three supporting sentences.
☐ Each paragraph of the body has a conclusion sentence.

Conclusion

☐ My conclusion has at least three sentences.
☐ My conclusion restates my main idea.
☐ My conclusion answers the question, "So what?"

Unity

☐ My essay flows well and makes sense.
☐ My essay uses transition words.
☐ My essay is interesting.

Subject Matter

☐ My essay has different sentences – short, long, compound, complex.
☐ My essay uses descriptive words.
☐ All parts of my essay support my main idea.

Grammar/Mechanics

☐ All words are spelled correctly.
☐ There are no grammatical mistakes.
☐ There are no punctuation errors.
☐ There are no fragments.
☐ There are no run-on sentences.

Read through your book report and fix any mistakes. Here is an editing checklist. Aim for a check mark in each box.

Introduction

☐ My introduction begins with an attention grabber.
☐ My introduction has at least three sentences.
☐ My introduction ends with the main idea of my essay.

Body

☐ The body of my essay has at least three paragraphs.
☐ Each paragraph of the body starts with a topic sentence.
☐ Each paragraph of the body has at least three supporting sentences.
☐ Each paragraph of the body has a conclusion sentence.

Conclusion

☐ My conclusion has at least three sentences.
☐ My conclusion restates my main idea.
☐ My conclusion answers the question, "So what?"

Unity

☐ My paper flows well and makes sense.
☐ My paper uses transition words.
☐ My paper is interesting.

Subject Matter

☐ My paper has different sentences – short, long, compound, complex.
☐ My paper uses descriptive words.
☐ All parts of my paper support my main idea.

Grammar/Mechanics

☐ All words are spelled correctly.
☐ There are no grammatical mistakes.
☐ There are no punctuation errors.
☐ There are no fragments.
☐ There are no run-on sentences.

Underline the adjectives in the sentences below. If you need help, try to find the nouns first, and then underline the words that are describing them. There are multiple adjectives in each sentence.

The small, yippy dog barked well into the summer night.

The young mom brought her newborn baby to the doctor.

My helpful brother will happily carry your heavy bags.

Whose striped bag is sitting on the filthy floor?

Stephanie lost her purple ring after three months.

The baby zebra galloped across the dusty terrain.

That dog has beautiful fur.

The colorful graphics made the computer game extra fun.

The popcorn ceiling left white flakes in my hair as I painted it.

My cozy bed is loudly calling my name at the end of this day.

We had a delicious dinner of juicy steak and mashed potatoes.

The quick brown fox jumped over the lazy dog.

The colorful leaves fell to the cold ground in the gentle breeze.

Draw your main character for a funny story you are going to write. Use the lines to write a bit about him or her. Make sure to give your character a name and age.

_____

_____

_____

_____

_____

Lesson 83: Funny Story

Use these three boxes to plot out your funny story. What's going to happen in the beginning, middle, and end?

_____

_____

_____

_____

_____

_____

_____

_____

_____

_____

_____

_____

The following chart is one way to brainstorm. You can remember the steps using the acronym FIRES. Fill in the chart below as it pertains to your persuasive essay.

	Topic 1	Topic 2	Topic 3
Facts			
Incidents			
Reasons			
Examples			
Statistics			

Lesson 162: Editing Checklist

Read through your essay and fix any weak spots. Here is your editing checklist again. Remember to aim for a check mark in each box.

Introduction
☐ My introduction begins with an attention grabber.
☐ My introduction has at least three sentences.
☐ My introduction ends with the main idea of my essay.

Body
☐ The body of my essay has at least three paragraphs.
☐ Each paragraph of the body starts with a topic sentence.
☐ Each paragraph of the body has at least three supporting sentences.
☐ Each paragraph of the body has a conclusion sentence.

Conclusion
☐ My conclusion has at least three sentences.
☐ My conclusion restates my main idea.
☐ My conclusion answers the question, "So what?"

Unity
☐ My essay flows well and makes sense.
☐ My essay uses transition words.
☐ My essay is interesting.

Subject Matter
☐ My essay has different sentences – short, long, compound, complex.
☐ My essay uses descriptive words.
☐ All parts of my essay support my main idea.

Grammar/Mechanics
☐ All words are spelled correctly.
☐ There are no grammatical mistakes.
☐ There are no punctuation errors.
☐ There are no fragments.
☐ There are no run-on sentences.

Use this sheet to record your resources, or the places where you find information for your final project. The info lines are short on purpose. Don't try to copy a full sentence. Take notes like "made in 1902" or "born on July 6." This will help you not copy what others wrote. Record the titles, authors, and dates of publication.

Topic:_____

Resource 1:_____

Info:_____ Info:_____

Info:_____ Info:_____

Info:_____ Info:_____

Resource 2:_____

Info:_____ Info:_____

Info:_____ Info:_____

Info:_____ Info:_____

Resource 3:_____

Info:_____ Info:_____

Info:_____ Info:_____

Info:_____ Info:_____

Lesson 168: Final Project

Continue to gather your research. Use this sheet to record your resources and notes for your project. Remember that the info lines are short on purpose. Just take notes instead of copying full sentences. This will ensure your work is your own and not copied from someone else.

Resource 4:_____

Info:_____   Info:_____

Info:_____   Info:_____

Info:_____   Info:_____

Resource 5:_____

Info:_____   Info:_____

Info:_____   Info:_____

Info:_____   Info:_____

Resource 6:_____

Info:_____   Info:_____

Info:_____   Info:_____

Info:_____   Info:_____

This is your last lesson for researching and gathering facts. Look for any missing pieces you feel you have and jot your notes below.

Resource 7:_____

Info:_____   Info:_____

Info:_____   Info:_____

Info:_____   Info:_____

Resource 8:_____

Info:_____   Info:_____

Info:_____   Info:_____

Info:_____   Info:_____

Resource 9:_____

Info:_____   Info:_____

Info:_____   Info:_____

Info:_____   Info:_____

Read through your research project and fix any weak spots. Here is your editing checklist again. Remember to aim for a check mark in each box.

Introduction
- ☐ My introduction begins with an attention grabber.
- ☐ My introduction has at least three sentences.
- ☐ My introduction ends with the main idea of my project.

Body
- ☐ The body of my essay has at least five paragraphs.
- ☐ Each paragraph of the body starts with a topic sentence.
- ☐ Each paragraph of the body has at least three supporting sentences.
- ☐ Each paragraph of the body has a conclusion sentence.

Conclusion
- ☐ My conclusion has at least three sentences.
- ☐ My conclusion restates my main idea.
- ☐ My conclusion answers the question, "So what?"

Unity
- ☐ My project flows well and makes sense.
- ☐ My project uses transition words.
- ☐ My project is interesting.

Subject Matter
- ☐ My project has different sentences – short, long, compound, complex.
- ☐ My project uses descriptive words.
- ☐ All parts of my project support my main idea.

Grammar/Mechanics
- ☐ All words are spelled correctly.
- ☐ There are no grammatical mistakes.
- ☐ There are no punctuation errors.
- ☐ There are no fragments.
- ☐ There are no run-on sentences.

The Easy Peasy All-in-One Homeschool is a free, complete online homeschool curriculum. There are 180 days of ready-to-go assignments for every level and every subject. It's created for your children to work as independently as you want them to. Preschool through high school is available as well as courses ranging from English, math, science, and history to art, music, computer, thinking, physical education, and health. A daily Bible lesson is offered as well. The mission of Easy Peasy is to enable those to homeschool who otherwise thought they couldn't.

The Genesis Curriculum takes the Bible and turns it into lessons for your homeschool. Daily lessons include Bible reading, memory verse, spelling, handwriting, vocabulary, grammar, Biblical language, science, social studies, writing, and thinking through discussion questions.

The Genesis Curriculum uses a complete book of the Bible for one full year. The curriculum is being made using both Old and New Testament books. Find us online at genesiscurriculum.com to read about the latest developments in this expanding curriculum.

Made in the USA
Monee, IL
26 August 2021